The Cottage on the Hill

Rustin Larson

Contents

The Cottage on the Hill

Bears and brownies and sour
disgraced elves lived there
high on the hill
a mile distant.
I could see their brown shuttered
cottage through the mists of a shattered
April struggling
with impulses of ice and snow
and cloud and sun and daffodil.
The bears dug landscape gardens,
loaded wheelbarrows full
with black dirt.
The brownies served orange pekoe
and almond ginger bread windmills.
The sour elves wrote
pages of unrhymed verse,
groused
about how small the world of fairies had become.
I kept an eye out from
a chair shoved to the room's window,
focused father's night watch
binoculars on their arched wooden door
the enchanted dark year before
kindergarten.

Sombreros

To protect us from the sun
as we stocked our garden
with seedlings of green bean,
bell pepper, onion, tomato,
and chard. Sombreros woven
from straw, shaggy brim,
we had our hoes,
dug Vs of earth,
sad little trenches, measured with
yard sticks, clawed out
weeds, shouldered the staffs
of rakes like rifles. Sombreros
kept our brains from cooking.
Sombreros licked the sweat
above our eyes,
buffered our necks from burning
bacon crisp. We remember sombreros
the way we remember clouds,
rain that fed us,
butter that anointed us,
cider that slaked our thirst.

That's Going to Take Some Time

Like a dog or religion or an
accident, a trombone
played on the radio to applause—
Rimsky-Korsacov
apple sauce,
you can't hear
more than you can hear.
You only have to wait
like a planet
no one knows is there:
the blue light of dawn
blackens the locust branches:
the cats claw at the ghost's chair
and sleep near the tree:
blue, red, green, over and over:
silent as April snowfall:
the elder cat returns to bed
and rests upon my hand.

Sarah with Her Tea

in her tiny wedge apartment
on a mild day, October 18, 2017,
a day after her birthday,
trees dancing behind her
framed by the window
princess crayons scattered
on her mattress

come draw with me she said
I get lonely here
because she works at the cafe down the hill
because she has bad luck with them

I draw her as she sits
Bodhisattva, lotus posture,
in her window, tea in her hand,
smiling because I came to visit
and she is not lonely

because God gave me three children
to make not lonely
as I and the sun both get older

Roaring Guitar

Brenda drives to install
the land line. She thinks
medical masks are bullshit.
She scared a scarred
family of rabbits when she
kicked the junction box. My
guitar isn't the red head beauty
she was fifty years ago, but she
sounds like an angel with steel
strings. I play a song about
someone riding a night train.
Brenda drives with cables and phone
lines in her hand. What do I do now?
I didn't load up the cereal bowls
so I'll have to use a mug for
Cheerios. Viruses are scary.
Quiet you birds, people are trying
to meditate! Copenhagen sounds
like a virus too. People asked
me to stop playing. It was
ruining their mantras.

Trolls

I missed a whole day. Now
three men with a metal detector
are digging outside my apartment
for precious metals. They swing
pick axes like mountain trolls,
giggle like girls in a crosswalk
outside the gymnasium. I left
my ability to walk on the ground
in Korea in 1952. I missed a
whole day. Someone tried to send
me a message. I woke and saw
a headless angel at the foot of
my bed. She wore white robes
and held up her arms like
the savior chanting "Peace
be with thee." My heart skipped
beats. My coffee cooled in a small white
cup like they used at Joe's in
1974 before the Hell's Angels kicked
their Harley's into life and left town
for the last time ever. The mountain
trolls laugh at their discovery of a
bag of "medicine" beneath the ground
outside my dirty apartment. They
hop in the black pickup truck
and drive far into the tornado warning.

Switcheroo

My shoes don't laugh, they list
to starboard like torpedoed
merchant marines. The CO
detector peels off one beep.
The landlord said this would be
the new normal. My handwriting
becomes disturbingly kempt
as if I transformed into a woman
in 1966, someone who never
missed a day or arrived late
at Bankers Life, hopping off
the transit at her stop at
Younker's department
store and scowling at me,
her other life, the teenage boy
who sits cross-legged in front of the
window display of autumn
coats, smokes Marlboro reds,
chews on his fingernails.

Not Until You're Happy and Fully Fortified

There are a lot of things I can
not do now that I want to do now
and could have done before all this
mess happened. I can't be-
lieve I would actually write
a sentence like that in a different
world. This had been science
fiction back in 1972. You see what
I mean? I'm going to make a turkey
chili dog for lunch; I can do that.
I can eat calmly and ignore all
the sounds I can hear as if ghosts
were whispering and flags were
fluttering over ancient graves
on a day of picnics and trembling
and black pills in little glass jars
on an oak dresser with necklaces
of river pearls and bowls of clam-shell
buttons, naked. Name time
and type a letter on an index card.
Eat orange sherbet from a cardboard
tube. Tie your worm to the hook
and shiver near the river pierced
in the sun. Your radio is swearing.
This is not the world you expected.

The Tremolo of Guitars

In the morning, I forgot my jacket at the old
house, so I got cold.
But later the sun got hot,
and the motorcycle helmets of miniature robots
lay scattered below the walnut
tree. Kids set up Kool-Aid
stands as the bikini girl
sunned herself on a towel
on her front lawn. Her
blue boyfriend owned
a Danelectro baritone with Vegas dice
tuning keys. We danced surf
moves on the front porch
clad only in our skivvies, but we were five
and received no criticism
except for Diane, also five, who joined us
in a shirtless go-go. Mother Mary, Joseph,
and Jesus, Mrs. Hess screamed
from across the flooded ditches.
Her cherry trees bled a gummy maroon
sap. We ate it and saw visions
of dragonflies skimming ponds
overflowing with Orange Tang. Astronauts
shot themselves
to the moon unafraid,
but unknown to everyone on earth,
a distant galaxy was assassinated
in gorgeous explosions of gold.

The Midway

The acne-skinned repair diggers
are at it again outside my apartment.
My knuckles feel like poison ivy,
but only because I have been washing
them so much for Covid-19. Still
people go on to their parking
lot, their grilled chicken and frankfurters
on such a fine day with the escalator
to the sky in full swing with tens
of thousands of new riders. I can
see a red and white football when
I close my eyes, and the repair diggers
have found geodes to crack open
with hammers, and just now I want
to hear a train's whistle, but I hear
nothing, like the day I was stranded
at Montpelier Junction with Mrs.
Electro and her husband, Jonquil, with
their portable bar and velvet carry-on luggage. I read
A Moveable Feast and ate cheese and
crackers in coach class, while
they road south in their port-a-room
to a meeting at the Algonquin
with their publisher, Sam the one-eyed diplomat.

Mr. Coffee

America, even with your dirty hands
tied behind your back, you scare
the fuck out of me. Even your
skies will drop a tornado
for a nasty look. You goddamn
misanthrope! To make up,
you gave us, Mr. Coffee. Thanks.
It's a humid Saturday in May
and my dental work throbs because
of Mr. Coffee. Mr. Coffee makes
my eyes tear at the sight of
lumpy clouds. Rita B. Marino
flips her cumulus skirts and dances and
shows us all how it's done. We are
allowed to read only Mary Oliver
and Billie Collins and believe what
we create must return to the soil
or decay fluttering in the branches
of trees. I'm dreary. An ant crawls
on my pillow. You don't count
Gerald Stern. You are not Bill & Mary.
Go home! I used to play marbles with
Jerry Stern when we were kids. I stole
all his cat's eyes. He cried like a
poopy diaper. So there you have it,
Angel. You can create America, but
you can't create the world, and by
world I mean Earth, and I say it
like a dirty double dealing Earthling.

Submarine

I am Captain of the 13c of
the Utopian fleet. ACHTUNG!!
My hot water is on the blink
again. S.O.S. Save our soy
sauce and our Liquid Aminos.
I believe in the all-one-god faith,
the communion of sinners, and
the resurrection of the baby.
I believe in the lost cat of my
soul, a lemon tabby, who is
never lost. I hoist a flagon in
your general direction. I am about
to abandon myself on your door-
step lest I go down with the
ship, my scallop, my scallion, and
my rusty skupper. Arrrrr, by
the crust of me scrod! I feels
a bitter wind a-blowin' the skies!
DIVE! DIVE! Up periscope!
DAS TORPEDO LOS! Sink
that cargo of Dollar Tree aspirin
and hair clips. A bloody conflagration
blackens the heaving of the troubled seas!

Monday

A cup of coffee tastes
like instant pencil shavings. The Italian
circus plays the sprightliest tunes
of FM radio. Rabbits congregate
glumly on the rugby pitch. I don't

know. My heart is a medicine
cabinet. The team has changed its
name to "The Shakespeares." The
robotic arm gleefully crushes another
garbage can and drives onto the

pixie surprise of the purple finches.
"Big smile" says the cardboard box
sitting across from me in the brown
chair. My mother-in-law says corn
tastes the same as always. She advises

my wife to pull the gold crowns from
my mouth if money becomes scarce. I feel
like a corpse in Poland. Sliver of
sun, can you part the clouds like
a bullet proof vest? Why are the

robins screaming? If I fail
to type this page, will you type it
for me? We once shared date-nut
cookies and stared into each other's eyes.

Before the Pandemic

There had been no place to go but up and that got to be a real mess in Wu-Han China in 1933 the first television prototype was developed this version did not rely upon cameras but instead produced pictures from random thought waves transmitted from the brains of anonymous individuals across the globe the device picking up everything from ships at sea classified state secrets and vaudeville acts to Cab Calloway singing Reefer Man in Sanskrit a woman chirps "go on the other side let me out let me out" this never sees full scale production the war interrupts civilization set scurrying like a barnyard in crisis foxes and coyotes leaping in and negative like the blood of lettuce and kale you thought it was some grand origami a luxury liner of folded paper there were quills lodged in the dog's muzzle and he cried in misery the aorta washed squeaky clean I'm looking for something to buoy me water hushes from the faucet in particular chemist fighting dew drowsiness and forecast folded prayers for me the apron hanging like a signal from the line hobo language a generous lady lives here my legs in a dance they can't find truly in language that means private action and a responsible keeper of responsibility and jail the cleanliness of it they'll do anything to make you feel inferior it's human nature we all have our moments of retardation and hallelujah now focus your attention on the paint store the colors there is a break which means a sentence of your own time is yours out of necessity I couldn't believe it when your letter arrived there it was confirmation of all I had been thinking but had been unable to say clearly with choice and or the best socks from the laundry bless you for trying pie in the sky blue Labradors and nausea which by the way has something to do with the ocean inside us evolution couldn't out the hen house windows of fire breaking out in the horse barn and Mrs. McCoy shrieking over apple pies we could have been the story predictably mankind becoming its own monster then as well but let's

die for our rights to cigarettes alcohol and Las Vegas too big it's right
here in recent memory you are standing upon it let's round out the level
of the wine glass like the interior of a stone the pony trots with broken
butter pots window eye tabla the sound of the sun rising

Village of the Dead

On a mountain hillside somewhere
there is a scattering of stone huts
unchanged since the year 1346.
The black death came and people's
houses quickly became their
personal mausoleums. They are
still inside. The sun rises, the daisies
grow, and it is unlucky for the living
to visit even for a short time.
Today in my town of 9000 souls
the dentists sweat and curse
for lack of patients. Gas stations
offer bargain bottom prices
for fuel to excursions to other villages.
The sun peeps through the clouds
for seven and one half seconds.
The river clears itself of pollution.
White-tail deer wander on the lawns
and sidewalks and quietly approach
the cottages and peer into the windows.

Print Notice

As a matter of fact, no. The princess
ball will not be held.
Focus on being closer to God.
There is a kernel of popcorn
on the floor. Jimmy Stevens
and the Scarecrows have canceled.
I am ready to go with the crystal
ball, the magic. I will commit
urination on the toilet seat.
The birds are a tragic argument
let it suffice to say. For cry I.
Good gravy, Virgil. Boiled potatoes
just like Hitler's mamma made.
The trolley cars clang like hammers
and scythes in Munich. The dentist
brushes his teeth in the mirror.
He was gassed during the great war.
The uniforms march now without
bodies to support them and die
in a heap at the Chinese laundry.
It is the morning the newsman
gives long explanations about
the flowers at the state funeral,
how each petal is a separate language
and is the purview of diplomats.
None-the-less the terriers
have the run of the market.

888

Secret area code. Survivalist compound
in the center of Mountain A.
The air has turned red and smells
like cherries. Mother Goose is cooked.
Pack the station wagon full of ice
water and run. This ain't no good.
I'm skeered, Marshall Dillon. Taint no one
on the side o' justice no more.
I stand like a hungry kid looking
through the bakery window at all
the brownie balls and apricot
kolacky. Soviet era rain jackets
adorn the lovely shoulders of the museum
staff. I eat sausage in the Czech Village
in the record heat. I dowse my thirst
with iced tea. We wear masks when
we are not eating to keep the spread
of the virus down. Rhesus monkeys rattle
cups of pennies at us. The sun is as bright
as a new law from an insane king.
The folk dancers circle each other
with rusted swords and ancient muskets.
It's precisely the festival we've been
praying for; the corn judge swings
from the shady branches; the temple
of garnets expels an avalanche
of red stones for the eyes of rats.

I Hear the Roar of Many Scary Creatures

My awareness floats six inches
from the grave
I watch the activity of black ants
and their red cousins
a rabbit flops and lounges in the mud
at my side
I hover I float I listen
to the chimes of distant children
who tinkle like breaking ice
but in the middle of summer
with extravagant mothers
mourning for their boys
who are not allowed to play baseball
against the ridiculous germs
the women hug their ownership
of the flesh
Chevy three on the wheel
down the gravel path to catastrophe
straight into the river of the unborn
and grandmother smacks a metal pan loudly
with a ladle because of catfish fried
and the trees are a tunnel of darkened cloud
and there are black raspberries
and mulberries and poisonous mushrooms
and rainwater stagnating in ditches
as the boys and men walk home
in mud-covered boots from the nearby fields
hairy legs sunburned cheeks
because they are their mother's flesh
which she owns

To My Surprise

The begonia plays hide and seek
with the Christmas cactus. I
calculate. Outside my door, a
rabbit waits, wrinkling its nose
and winking at me. It breathes
and the side of its body ripples,
beautiful, soft, shades of dry grass,
mud and fallen leaves. For a half
hour, I walk by the door and the
rabbit waits in the lawn path. When
I finally put on my jacket and
step outside, the rabbit is gone.
I walk to the mailbox and drop
the letter down the hatch. It has
been dark and cool two weeks now,
rainy all the time. I am quite
aware of my heart in my chest,
hopping, thumping, settling down again.